Vegan Snacks

23 Quick & Easy Recipes To Enjoy Delicious & Healthy Vegan Snacks

© **Copyright 2016 by Sef Hohenheim - All rights reserved.**

This document is geared towards providing exact and reliable information in regards to the topic and issue covered. The publication is sold with the idea that the publisher is not required to render accounting, officially permitted, or otherwise, qualified services. If advice is necessary, legal or professional, a practiced individual in the profession should be ordered.

- From a Declaration of Principles which was accepted and approved equally by a Committee of the American Bar Association and a Committee of Publishers and Associations.

In no way is it legal to reproduce, duplicate, or transmit any part of this document in either electronic means or in printed format. Recording of this publication is strictly prohibited and any storage of this document is not allowed unless with written permission from the publisher. All rights reserved.

The information provided herein is stated to be truthful and consistent, in that any liability, in terms of inattention or otherwise, by any usage or abuse of any policies, processes, or directions contained within is the solitary and utter responsibility of the recipient reader. Under no circumstances will any legal responsibility or blame be held against the publisher for any reparation, damages, or monetary loss due to the information herein, either directly or indirectly.

Respective authors own all copyrights not held by the publisher.

The information herein is offered for informational purposes solely, and is universal as so. The presentation of the information is without contract or any type of guarantee assurance.

The trademarks that are used are without any consent, and the publication of the trademark is without permission or backing by the trademark owner. All trademarks and brands within this book are for clarifying purposes only and are the owned by the owners themselves, not affiliated with this document.

Table of Contents

Introduction	1
What A Vegan Diet Is All About	2
Why Join The Vegan Movement	5
How To Maintain A Vegan Diet	8
Snack Recipes	10
1. Pumpkin Muffins	10
2. Baked Sweet Potato Chips	12
3. Pumpkin Chia Pudding with Vanilla Cream	13
4. Fresh fruit with Tangerine Cashew Cream	15
5. Papaya Chia Pudding	16
6. Roasted Garbanzo Beans	17
7. Baked Parsnip Chips	18
8. Baked Apple Chips With Cashew Dip	19
9. Lime Roasted Chickpeas	21
10. Tortilla Chips With Garbanzo Guacamole Dip	22
11. Steamed Broccoli with "Cheese"	23
12. Banana Muffins	24
13. Sweet Almonds	25
14. Chips And Vegan Hummus	26
15. Vegan Shake	27
16. Vegan Overnight Oats	28
17. Coconut Oat Parfait With Blueberry Jam	30

18.	Apple "Cupcakes"	32
19.	Peach Crumble	33
20.	Avocado snack	34
21.	Roasted Corn On The Cob	35
22.	Homemade Crackers	36
23.	Strawberry Oat Squares With Homemade Jam	38
Conclusion		40

Introduction

I want to thank you and congratulate you for purchasing the book, "Vegan Snacks - 23 Quick & Easy Recipes To Enjoy Delicious & Healthy Vegan Snacks".

This book contains proven steps and strategies on how to make easy and tasty vegan snacks.

Vegans miss out on many different foods. Heck, they miss out on many things: no franks or grilled burgers at picnics. No fries cooked in animal fat or turkey at thanksgiving dinner. Strict vegans may even take a rain check on honey.

But vegans also tend to less likely suffer from major health complications plagued by many people. They are more likely not to suffer from heart related ailments, and generally live longer than the rest of the population. However, the greatest challenge for many vegans is thinking that they don't have options especially when it comes to tasty snacks. Most think that the only snacks they can take are veggies like carrots, beets and fruits. You will be surprised to know that you have many options at your disposal.

This book will look at 23 tasty vegan snacks that will change your perception about vegan food. With these snacks, you don't have to worry about being vegan anymore. Now, you can make your vegan days more exciting by enjoying various delicious recipes and snack on them anytime you want.

What A Vegan Diet Is All About

Before we look at how you stand to benefit by following a vegan diet and some recipes, let us look at what a vegan diet is all about. Veganism is about not eating meat as well as animal products. Here are some staples for first-time vegans:

Healthy oils – Go for extra-virgin olive oil or try canola oil and flaxseed oil, which contain omega-3 fat that is good for your health.

Nuts and seeds – These are great to meet your protein and fat requirements. Nuts and seeds also contain iron, zinc, and vitamin E.

Tofu – This versatile meat substitute can be a valuable addition to your kitchen. You can bake, grill, fry, or sauté the tofu!

Seasonings – For a flavorful diet, you will need to stock on your seasoning. You can shop for cayenne, basil, paprika, kosher salt, curry powder, rosemary and more. You can buy this fresh at farmer's markets or specialty stores.

Faux Milk – This is a great whole milk substitute. You can also try rice milk and almond milk. In addition to it being a drink, you can also use it for cooking and baking.

Beans – Another popular staple food for vegan since it's rich in protein and is a versatile ingredient like tofu.

Whole grains – The best source of carbohydrates is whole grains. They are also packed with other essential nutrients like vitamin E, zinc, magnesium, iron, and B vitamins. Try oats, brown rice, quinoa, and whole-wheat pastas.

Vegetables and Fruits – Of course you can't go vegan without the veggies! If you want to save some money, then choose the ones in season, same as with your fruit selection for smoothies and desserts.

Tip: If you are trying to lose weight, avoid starchy vegetables whenever possible (potatoes, corns, green peas etc.). You can also go for organic products to avoid ingesting chemicals and increase the amount of vitamins, minerals, and essential fatty acids that your body can absorb. Eat them raw when possible for the maximum nutritional value possible. Since a vegan diet tends to eliminate other food groups from your diet, you have to make sure that you have a well-balanced meal plan in order to avoid any deficiencies. Here are some important nutrients that you need to ensure your diet has:

Protein and Amino Acids

Meat is high in protein, but it has alternative sources such as soy. You can meet your amino acids requirements by consuming whole grains, veggies, seeds, and nuts.

Iron - The richest source of iron is liver, egg yolk, and red meat, which are all high in cholesterol. To avoid iron deficiency, you can consume spinach, dried fruits, dried beans, chickpeas, pinto beans, whole wheat, parsley, fortified veggie burger, prunes, raisins and more. Another tip is to eat vitamin C rich food, since it helps in iron absorption. If you're low on iron, avoid taking zinc-rich foods at the same meal.

Calcium - Good sources of calcium include spinach, broccoli, soybean products, kale, sunflower seeds, okra, figs, oranges, almonds, flaxseed, pistachio nuts, chickpeas, non-dairy yoghurts, fortified breakfast cereals and more.

Zinc - This is another important nutrient for growth and development that can be found in legumes, nuts, and grains.

Omega 3 - Since seafood is out of the diet, you can take flax seeds/flax oil or omega 3 DHA supplements in the form of algae. This is very important especially for vegans who are breast-feeding, diabetic, or pregnant (At least 300 mg of DHA a day).

Now that you know what a vegan diet entails, let us now look at why you should adopt a vegan diet to give you some motivation to try out the vegan snacks in this book.

Why Join The Vegan Movement

Vegans are often misunderstood as preferential eaters with a rather bizarre passion for animal rights. While it is true that many vegans are arguably, more compassionate about animals, a vegan lifestyle and diet goes beyond ethics, and into the realms of health and nutrition. By simply adopting or following a vegan diet, you will enjoy a number of benefits. These include:

Better nutrition

You'll get all of the nutritional benefits explained below from adopting a vegan diet complete with foods such as soy products, beans, nuts, whole grains, fruits and vegetables.

Reduced saturated fats: meats and dairy products are high in saturated fats. You can improve your health significantly by cutting back on the amount of saturated fats you take.

Magnesium: Magnesium helps in the absorption of calcium, and it's role is often overlooked when it comes to a healthy diet. Excellent sources of magnesium include dark leafy greens, seeds, and nuts.

Fiber: This diet is rich in fiber (particularly found in vegetables and fruits), and promotes healthier bowel movement, making you feel healthy and light. Diets that are rich in fiber also help protect against colon cancer.

Antioxidants: These protect your body against cell damage caused by free radicals, which can ultimately lead to some forms of cancer. They are said to be very effective on the skin, making it look extremely radiant.

Vitamin E: This powerful vitamin is great for your brain, eyes, skin, and heart, and can even help protect against Alzheimer's disease. Vitamin E can be found in dark leafy greens, nuts, and grains.

Phytochemicals: These are found in plant-based foods, and can boost your protective enzymes, help prevent and protect your body against cancer, and support antioxidants in your body.

Protein: Most people tend to overdo on protein, and in some rather unhealthy ways in the form of red meat. It is interesting to note that the best sources of healthy protein are actually not animals. Excellent sources of vegan protein include soy products, lentils, peas, nuts, and beans.

Disease prevention

A healthy, balanced vegan diet has been shown to prevent several diseases, including, but not limited to the following:

Cardiovascular disease

Enhance your cardiovascular healthy by eating whole grains and nuts, while steering away from meat and dairy products. A certain British study even demonstrated that the vegan diet could reduce your risk of type II diabetes and heart disease. Vegan diet goes a long way towards preventing stroke and heart attack, especially by cutting back on cholesterol and saturated fats.

Cholesterol

When you eliminate any animal-based food from your diet, you automatically cut out all dietary cholesterol from your food.

Blood pressure

A diet that is based on whole grains is great for your health in several ways, but mainly in lowering high blood pressure.

Prostate cancer

A certain study revealed that men who were developing prostate cancer in the early stages, and then adopted a vegan diet either prevented the disease from progressing, or even reversed it in some cases.

Colon cancer

Taking a diet made up of whole grains, fresh fruits and vegetables can significantly reduce your risk of colon cancer.

Breast cancer

Women who take very little meat and animal products have been shown to have a lower rate of breast cancer than those who consume animal products liberally.

Macular degeneration

Diets that are high in fresh fruits and vegetables, particularly sweet potatoes, pumpkin, carrots, and leafy greens, can help you avoid macular degeneration associated with age.

One of the hardest things when adopting any kind of diet is sticking to it. Therefore, let us look at how to stick to the vegan diet and keep at it.

How To Maintain A Vegan Diet

After the transition from being a meat-eater to being a vegan, the next step is to stick to the vegan lifestyle. As you form and develop vegan habits, there are certain pitfalls that are bound to pull you back.

Here are some common mistakes that new vegans make and that you should avoid in order to stick to the diet:

Eating the same amount of food as your pre-vegan days

If you are always feeling hungry on your new diet, then you are doing it wrong. When it comes to plant-based food, you need to eat larger portions because you are now consuming fewer calories than before. Learn to check calorie content of your meals to determine if you are on the right track.

Not listening to your body

A new habit takes approximately 21 days to form. So let you body adjust and don't get discouraged if you are feeling a bit different or develop some craving. Listen to your body carefully - if you are hungry eat, and if you feel that you are not satisfied with what you are consuming, try out other dishes. You have to understand that your body or your system is undergoing major changes. Another tip here is to always stay hydrated – don't hold back on water!

Not checking out the labels

Be sure to check out all food labels, as some food tends to contain trivial and hidden amounts of animal products. On the other hand, lactose-free labeled products are not synonymous to non-dairy products.

Same diet every day

If you are eating the same food every day, you will be missing out on other essential vitamins and minerals. While eating a huge bowl of salad is not bad, taking it on a regular basis can make you miss out on other varieties of food. Variety is important on your diet to avoid any nutritional deficiencies or craving for other food. Learn some new recipes to make your health journey an enjoyable one.

Sticking to salad when eating out

Again, the vegan diet comes with several options. You can ask the restaurant for custom made vegan dishes or you can search for restaurants that can meet your requirements. Keep in mind that your nutrient requirements will differ when you're pregnant, lactating, or as you age.

Snack Recipes

1. Pumpkin Muffins

Yields 1 dozen

Ingredients

For the wet ingredients:

3 tablespoons water

1/3 cup of melted coconut oil or grape seed oil

½ cup packed brown sugar

1 tablespoon chia seeds

1 cup unsweetened pumpkin puree

3 tablespoons pure maple syrup

¼ cup blackstrap molasses

For the dry ingredients:

1 teaspoon baking soda

1 tablespoon pumpkin pie spice

1 2/3 cups whole-grain spelt flour

1 teaspoon baking powder

½ teaspoon fine sea salt

Heaping ½ cup of toasted chopped walnuts (optional)

Directions

- Preheat oven to 350 degrees F, and line a muffin pan with paper liners. Whisk together the water and chia seeds in a medium bowl, and then set aside.

- In a large bowl, mix the dry ingredients (baking powder, salt, baking soda, pumpkin pie spice, and spelt flour).

- Whisk the wet ingredients (molasses, brown sugar, maple syrup, oil, pumpkin puree, and chia mixture), into the bowl with the chia mixture until smooth.

- Stir the dry ingredients into the wet mixture until just incorporated. Ensure that you do not over mix the batter, since the spelt flour is very delicate.

- Stir the chopped walnuts into the batter, if using.

- Divide the batter 12 muffin liners.

- Bake in the preheated oven for twenty to twenty four minutes, or until an inserted toothpick comes out smoothly. Transfer the muffins into the pan for five to ten minutes to cool slightly, and then put on a cooling rack to cool completely. Serve with almond milk.

2. Baked Sweet Potato Chips

Serves 3

Ingredients

2 sweet potatoes, washed and dried thoroughly

2 tablespoons of olive oil

Black pepper

¼ tablespoon of sea salt

Directions

- Preheat oven to 250 degrees F. Cut the sweet potatoes uniformly as thin as possible. Put the sweet potato slices in a large bowl, and drizzle with olive oil. Toss to coat, and then sprinkle salt and pepper over. Toss again to combine.
- Arrange the slices over a baking sheet, in a single layer.
- Bake in the preheated oven for about two hours, flipping chips once a halfway. Make sure the slices are evenly cooked.
- Remove from oven once crisp and golden brown. Set aside to rest for ten minutes. Enjoy!

3. Pumpkin Chia Pudding with Vanilla Cream

Serves 1

Ingredients

Chia Layer

2 tablespoons of raw coconut cream

5 tablespoons of raw pumpkin juice

1 orange, juiced

1 teaspoon of extra virgin olive oil

3 drops of organic vanilla extract

5×1 cm fresh ginger root, peeled & grated

1 pinch cayenne pepper

3 handfuls of chia seeds

Matcha cream layer

2 tablespoons of brown rice syrup or preferred clear liquid sweetener

15 drops organic vanilla extract

3 tablespoons of raw coconut cream

½ teaspoon of matcha green tea powder

Directions

- To prepare the chia layer: combine the vanilla, cayenne, grated ginger root, coconut cream, orange juice, and pumpkin puree in a food processor. Blend until smooth, slowly adding in the olive oil.

- Combine the chia seeds and liquid in a bowl, and stir gently using a spatula or spoon. Transfer into a bowl or glass and leave to sit overnight or for an hour.

- To prepare the matcha cream: place the coconut cream, vanilla, sweetener, and matcha in a bowl. Whisk until smooth, and then pour over the chia layer. Optional: Freeze for thirty minutes to strengthen the cream a bit. Alternatively, sprinkle fresh mint over the top, and enjoy right away!

4. Fresh fruit with Tangerine Cashew Cream

Serves 2

Ingredients

Tangerine cashew cream

½ cup freshly squeezed tangerine juice

½ cup raw cashews soaked for ten minutes up to overnight, in water,

1 teaspoon of 100% maple syrup

Directions

- Drain cashews and combine with the maple syrup and tangerine juice in a blender. Blend on high setting until the mixture attains a smooth and creamy consistency.

- Pour this over fresh fruit and enjoy.

5. Papaya Chia Pudding

Serves 4

Ingredients

6 tablespoons chia seeds

1 teaspoons maple syrup

Squeeze of lemon

2 cups unsweetened almond milk

1 small papaya, peeled and sliced

Directions

- Combine the maple syrup, chia seeds, and almond milk in a glass container, and stir thoroughly until chia seeds are properly mixed in. Place in the refrigerator for a few hours, or until the chia seeds expand.

- Drizzle the lemon juice over the sliced papaya. Transfer the pudding into a bowl, and top with the papaya. Drizzle a bit of maple syrup. Enjoy

6. Roasted Garbanzo Beans

Serves 2

Ingredients

1 ½ tablespoons of olive oil

Preferred spice blend

1 (15-ounce) can of garbanzo beans

Salt

Directions

- Preheat oven to 400 degrees F. Drain the garbanzo beans into a strainer, and then rinse for a few seconds with running water to clean the beans. Get rid of the excess water using a strainer.

- Spread the beans over a paper towel lined baking sheet. Place another paper towel over the layer of beans to absorb any remaining water. Wrap the beans around the paper towel to remove any thin skin from the beans. Throw away the paper towels and skins.

- Coat the beans with the olive oil, and roast in the preheated oven for thirty to forty minutes, or until crunchy and golden brown. Season with spice blend and salt.

7. Baked Parsnip Chips

Serves 8

Ingredients

3 parsnips, washed with skin on

Olive oil

Black pepper

Salt or garlic salt

Directions

- Preheat oven to 350 degrees F. Cut the parsnips into 1/8 inch thick pieces. Put the parsnips slices in a large bowl, and drizzle with olive oil. Toss to coat, and then sprinkle salt and pepper over. Toss again to combine.

- Arrange the slices over two silicone lined baking sheets, in a single layer. Don't overlap.

- Bake in the preheated oven for fifteen minutes, or until the edges curl and the middle is firm. Remove from oven and set aside to cool. Enjoy!

8. Baked Apple Chips With Cashew Dip

Yields about 40 chips and 2 ½ cups dip

Ingredients

Apple chips

2 apples

1 lemon

Cinnamon to taste and dust chips

1 cup of water

Cashew cinnamon dip

1 medium cored apple, quartered

1 teaspoon cinnamon

Salt to taste

1 cup raw cashews

1 tablespoon agave nectar

½ cup water

Directions

- Soak the cashews in a bowl of water, and leave to sit overnight, or for several hours at least.
- Preheat oven to 200 degrees F, and then line two large baking sheets with parchment paper. Combine the water with the lemon squeeze in a glass bowl.

- Using a sharp knife or mandolin, cut the apples into thin slices, and then dip the in the bowl with the lemon and water mixture. Arrange them on the lined baking sheet, side by side. Sprinkle cinnamon over the top, and bake in the oven for ninety minutes. Flip the slices, and then remove the apples from oven when crisp, about three hours.

- Meanwhile, drain the cashews and then combine them with the cinnamon, agave nectar, and quartered apple in a food processor or speed blender. Gently add in the water until the mixture achieves a smooth consistency. Season with some salt then serve with the chips.

9. Lime Roasted Chickpeas

Serves 4-6

Ingredients

2 teaspoons lime infused olive oil

2 cans organic garbanzo beans

2 tablespoons of Mexican seasoning

Directions

- Preheat oven to 425 degrees F. Rinse the garbanzo beans properly, and then pass through a strainer.

- Transfer into a mixing bowl, and then stir in the olive oil. Add the Mexican seasoning, and stir until coated. Distribute the chickpeas evenly on a 9X13" cake pan.

- Bake in the oven for fifteen minutes, open, stir, and then bake for another fifteen minutes.

10. Tortilla Chips With Garbanzo Guacamole Dip

Serves 6

Ingredients

1 organic lemon, juiced

2 teaspoons of extra virgin olive oil

Sea salt and pepper to taste

1 cup of cooked & cooled garbanzo beans

A pinch of fresh organic cilantro

½ organic avocado

Tortilla chips

Directions

- Mix all the ingredients (apart from the cilantro and tortilla chips) in a medium mixing bowl, and then transfer to a serving bowl. Add the fresh cilantro over the top and enjoy with tortilla chips!

11. Steamed Broccoli with "Cheese"

Serves 4

Ingredients

3-4 tablespoons of runny tahini

2 teaspoons of dark red wine balsamic vinegar

1 teaspoon of garlic powder

1 teaspoon of fine sea salt

½- ¾ cup of water, as needed

2 heaping tablespoons of tomato paste

¼- ½ cup of nutritional yeast

1 teaspoon of onion powder

2 cups steamed broccoli florets

Directions

Process all the ingredients in a blender or food processor until thick, about thirty seconds. If you are not using any of these machines, just whisk all the ingredients in a bowl until thick. Add any toppings of your choice, for example chili powder or jalapenos to spice up the "cheese". Serve this with the broccoli

12. Banana Muffins

Yields 14 muffins

Ingredients

2 cups packed baby spinach

1 ½ cups whole-wheat flour

1 teaspoon baking soda

1/8 teaspoon salt

3 ripe bananas

8 strawberries

¾ cup sugar

¼ cup canola oil

1 teaspoon of cinnamon

Directions

- Preheat oven to 350°F, and then puree the strawberries, spinach, and bananas in a blender. Combine the baking soda, oil, sugar, flour, salt, and cinnamon in a bowl. Transfer the smoothie mixture into the bowl, and stir well.

- Arrange silicone or paper muffin cups in a muffin pan.

- Spoon the batter into the cups, filling each muffin cup up to ¾ full. Bake in the preheated oven for twenty to thirty minutes, or until inserted toothpick comes out smoothly.

13. Sweet Almonds

Serves 4

Ingredients

1 cup of whole raw almonds

½ - 1 tablespoon of maple syrup

1 teaspoon of liquid smoke

Few shakes of sea salt

Directions

- Preheat oven to 425 degrees F. Stir together the liquid smoke and syrup in a small cup. In a small bowl, mix the liquid and the almond until evenly coated. Pour the almonds onto a parchment paper lined baking sheet, and distribute them evenly. Bake for five minutes, and then remove the pan. Stir the almonds using a spatula or rubber spoon, and then return into the oven for another two minutes.

- Remove from oven and serve onto a plate immediately. Break the almonds apart as they cool, and then store in the refrigerator until ready to serve.

14. Chips And Vegan Hummus

Serves 6-8

Ingredients

1¼ cups of tomato puree/sauce

1 tablespoon of dried oregano

1 teaspoon of garlic powder

2 tablespoons of lemon juice

2 (15 oz.) cans of garbanzo beans, drained & rinsed thoroughly

1 teaspoon of fine sea salt

1 tablespoon of dried basil

½ teaspoon of red pepper flakes

2 tablespoons of runny tahini

Your favorite chips

Optional toppings: fresh basil, olives, red pepper flakes

Directions

- Drain and rinse out the beans, and then process in a food processor until mashed and broken up. Pour in the tomato puree, and continue blending until very smooth.
- Mix in the other ingredients, and puree until completely smooth. Adjust the spices, if needed, and then serve in a bowl with your favorite toppings. Serve with your favorite chips and enjoy!

15. Vegan Shake

Serves 1-2

Ingredients

1 cup frozen banana

8 fluid ounces Silk Almond Milk Vanilla Singles

1 cup fresh spinach

¼ cup avocado, chopped

4 to 6 Fresh Mint Leaves

Optional

1 teaspoon Cacao Nibs

1 cup ice

Directions

- Combine all the ingredients (except for the cacao nibs) in a blender, and process until smooth. Toss in the ice, if using, and process until it forms a thick and creamy consistency.

- Garnish with additional mint leaves and the cacao nibs, and enjoy!

16. Vegan Overnight Oats

Serves 1

Ingredients

2 tablespoons of chia seeds

½ cup of gluten-free rolled oats

¼ teaspoon of pure vanilla extract (optional)

1 large ripe/spotty banana, mashed

¼ teaspoon of cinnamon

¾ cup of almond milk

Toppings:

Fresh fruit

Pure maple syrup

Nuts and seeds

Granola

Coconut flakes

Cinnamon

Banana soft serve

Directions

- Mash the banana in a small bowl until roughly smooth. Stir in the cinnamon and chia seeds until combined. Mix in the vanilla, almond milk, and oats, and then put in the refrigerator while covered for two hours, or overnight.

- Stir the mixture to combine. If it still has a runny consistency, simply mix in one more tablespoon of chia seeds into the mixture, and return to the refrigerator until thick.

17. Coconut Oat Parfait With Blueberry Jam

Serves 4-6

Ingredients

For the blueberry chia seed jam:

¼ cup of pure maple syrup

3 tablespoons of chia seeds

550g of frozen blueberries

Dash of fine sea salt

1 teaspoon of fresh lemon juice, or to taste

For the vegan overnight oats:

1 cup rolled oats

1 tablespoon of pure maple syrup

¼ teaspoon of cinnamon, or to taste

1 (15 oz) can of full-fat coconut milk

3 tablespoons of chia seeds

½ teaspoon of ground cardamom , or to taste

1-2 small ripe pears, diced

Directions

- **To make the chia seed jam**: Mix together the maple syrup and blueberries in a medium pot until incorporated. Season with salt, and simmer over medium heat, without the lid, for eight to ten minutes, or until soft.

- Stir in the chia seeds, and continue simmering while stirring often for about eight to fifteen minutes more, or until the jam diminishes in volume and most of the water has evaporated.

- Remove from heat, and add the lemon juice. Put the mixture into a bowl, and cool in the refrigerator for a couple of hours. You can also slide the jam into your freezer for about forty five to sixty minutes, for quicker cooling.

- ***For the vegan oats***: Stir together the cinnamon, cardamom, maple syrup, chia seeds, oats, and coconut milk in a medium bowl or medium container until combined. Cover and chill for one to two hours, or until the mixture thickens and the oats are soft. Stir to combine.

- Layer the diced pea, overnight oats, and chia jam inside small jars, and secure with lids. Store the leftovers in the refrigerator for up to three to four days.

18. Apple "Cupcakes"

Serves 1-2

Ingredients

2 tablespoons almond butter

1 medium apple

Chocolate chips, dried fruit, cacao nibs, nuts or unsweetened coconut for topping

Directions

- Slice the apples into small discs, and top each with the nut butter for frosting. Sprinkle your favorite toppings over the top and enjoy!

19. Peach Crumble

Serves 4

Ingredients

½ cup of Medjool dates, pitted & chopped

4 ripe peaches, sliced into ¼ inch thick

1 teaspoon of fresh ginger, grated

2 teaspoons of maple syrup

Dash of cinnamon

1½ cup of pecans

Pinch of sea salt

Directions

- Combine the maple syrup with the sliced peaches, and toss to combine

- Pulse the ginger, dates, pecans, salt and cinnamon in a food processor until it forms a hearty crumble. Combine the sliced peaches with this crumble, and then serve into a pie dish.

20. Avocado snack

Serves 1

Ingredients

1 medium lavash wrap

1 teaspoon of agave syrup or maple syrup

½ teaspoon virgin coconut oil

½ medium avocado, sliced

Pinch sea salt

Directions

- Put coconut oil in a skillet and melt over high heat. Warm and loosen the lavash wrap for one minute. Remove from the heat then add the sliced avocado in a single layer over the warm lavash. Fold the warm lavash into 1/3 to cover the avocado.

- Spread the sweetener over the top to coat, and then flip once. Season with salt, and slice to serve.

21. Roasted Corn On The Cob

Serves 4

Ingredients

1 lime sliced into half & seeds removed

1½ teaspoons salt or more to taste

4 ears of corn

1 teaspoon cayenne/red chili powder or more to taste

¼ teaspoon cumin powder

Other additions:

¼ teaspoon chaat masala, amchoor (dry mango powder), kala namak (Indian black salt), or more to taste

- *Directions*
- Separate the strings and cornhusk from the corn, and then roast the corn over open gas flame or on the grill at medium heat, turning it around every thirty seconds.
- Combine all the spices in a bowl, and then dip half a lime into this mixture. Rub over the corn, and serve hot.

22. Homemade Crackers

Makes 60 crackers

Ingredients

1 ½ tablespoons sugar

¼ teaspoon paprika

¼ cup + 2 tablespoons of water

1 ¼ cups (5 oz) of 100% whole wheat flour

½ teaspoon salt + extra for sprinkling on

4 tablespoons of Earth Balance or butter

¼ teaspoon of vanilla

Directions

- Preheat oven to 400 degrees F. Line 2 baking sheets with nonstick mat or parchment paper.

- Mix the dry ingredients (paprika, sugar, flour, salt) in a large bowl. Cut the earth balance using a pastry blender and stir into the flour mixture until it forms a crumbly consistency.

- Mix the vanilla and water together, and then add into the Earth balance and flour mixture. Stir until properly combined.

- Divide the dough into two, and then roll one-half over a nonstick mat or floured surface. Cut the dough into your preferred shape using a pizza cutter. Layer the crackers over the lined baking sheet using a spatula. Add more sesame seeds and salt, as desired.

- Bake for eight to ten minutes, rotating the pan halfway through the baking to ensure it bakes evenly, about ten minutes. Set aside to cool completely, and then store in an airtight container.

23. Strawberry Oat Squares With Homemade Jam

Makes 12-16 squares

Ingredients

For Oat Base

1 cup of whole-grain flour (or blend of whole wheat and white flour)

½ teaspoon of sea salt

1 chia egg

¼ cup of pure maple syrup

1 tablespoons of sesame seeds

1 ½ cups regular oats

½ teaspoon of baking soda

½ cup brown sugar

½ cup plus 2 tablespoons Earth Balance, melted

2 tablespoons of almond milk

For Strawberry Jam

3-4 tablespoons of sugar, to taste

2 ¼ cups of chopped strawberries, cut into half inch pieces

1 tablespoon of chia seeds

Directions

- Preheat oven to 350 degrees F, and then line a 9X9 square pan with parchment paper. Spread the inside of the pan with oil. Mix the sugar and chopped strawberries in a medium pot, and heat over low heat until the strawberries start sweating. Stir in the chia seeds, and then bring the mixture to a boil. Now, simmer over medium low heat for about ten minutes, or until thick. Remove from heat, and then set aside to cool for five to ten minutes.

- In a small bowl, combine the flax egg or chia, then mix and set aside. Mix the dry ingredients for the oat base in a large bowl: salt, baking soda, brown sugar, flour, and oats. In a small bowl, mix the chia egg, almond milk, maple syrup, and melted earth balance.

- Combine the wet mixture (set half a cup aside) to the dry ingredients, and stir to combine. Transfer the oat mixture into the pan, and use your fingers to press it down. Smoothen it out using a pastry roller, if necessary. Spread over the strawberry mixture, and then top with the reserved half cup of oat mixture. Sprinkle one tablespoon of coconut or sesame seeds over the top.

- Bake in the oven for about thirty minutes, and then set aside to cool for about thirty to forty minutes. Slice and store in the fridge in a plastic container to keep it firm. Serve with your favorite dip.

Conclusion

Thank you again for purchasing this book!

I hope this book was able to help you to know that there are actually tasty vegan snacks you can try.

The next step is to try out the recipes and you will not be disappointed.

Thank you and enjoy!

Made in the USA
Monee, IL
19 December 2020